Structured Thoughts
And Fond Memories

Haiku Poetry

Dick Shultz

R. Shultz

6/28/2022

THE AUTHOR

Dick Shultz, a very happily semi-retired employee benefits insurance agent, has found a new passion in haiku poetry. In between bike rides, over the past six months, he has found the inspiration to create these poems.

God works his wonders in mysterious ways! One of his mom's favorite sayings. It's so true. Upon reading a book of haiku poetry his creative side was awakened and this book is the result.

If not for small, seemingly unimportant blessings in our lives we may never have known, become, believed, forgiven, or paid it forward.

Thanks to this blessing, Dick has this opportunity to share his faith, presented in a thought provoking manner within a precise structure.

Of course, some "whimsy" poetry, as he calls it, is merely meant to entertain.

The author may be contacted at 2shultz@sbcglobal.net

THANK YOU!

Sam Gutierrez

Not only did Sam provide the inspiration for this project by encouraging me to write my own poetry, he said that he would be "honored" that I wished to use a few of his poems, with words that I have added, in this book.

Sam also provided the guidance and technical expertise to help me get this project in the correct form for publication. He pulled together all the pieces and was the liaison with the publisher. My gratitude is beyond measure!

Kevin Adams, Sam Gutierrez

The Sunday morning messages from these two pastors at Granite Springs Church in Lincoln, California provided many sources of inspiration that helped me formulate my thoughts and ideas into poetry.

Brad Franklin, Sean Miller and John Voelz

These three pastors at Lakeside Church in Folsom, California also provided me with inspiration for several poems in this project. Thank you for offering uplifting messages that are both thought provoking and so meaningful in daily life.

Nancy Shultz

The keeper of all things precious, my dear wife looked through many, many photo albums to find the pictures that I recalled from memory, but had no idea where to find. In addition, her daily encouragement to keep this project on track to fruition was a blessing.

FOREWORD

I was recently given two books of poetry composed by Sam Gutierrez, a Pastor at Granite Springs Church, Lincoln California. As I read and reread these poems I became intrigued by the haiku style which Sam used in many of his poems. Some are quite short and I started to add my own words, also in the haiku style, to his poems.

One Sunday I summoned up the courage to share my first addition to one of his poems, titled "Virgin". Sam was very encouraging in his comments and suggested that I also try composing my own stories in the same haiku style. Sam's words of poetry are *italicized* and mine are not.

Haiku is a very simple structure for telling a story. The most common form of haiku has three lines with five syllables in the first line, seven in the second and five in the third. Precisely seventeen syllables in each verse. No iambic pentameter to be concerned with, just a simple structure that demands a lot of thought! There's one line of my poetry (not in italics) in this book that does not fit the haiku style. Maybe you can find it!

Over the past few months I have added more verses to some of Sam's poems. Sam has been very gracious in allowing me to use his original words as a prelude to my continuation of his poetic stories. Again, Sam's original verses are shown in italics, followed by my verses in regular type.

I encourage you to find Sam's books of poetry, which I have listed below, as they may also serve you with inspiration, both in the reading and perhaps in writing. They are available at Amazon.com.

"Read These Poems About David", poems by Sam Gutierrez
     www.amazon.com/poetry

"God Birth Poems", poems by Sam Gutierrez
     www.amazon.com/poetry

This book, "Structured Thoughts and Fond Memories," is also available at www.amazon.com/poetry

STRUCTURED THOUGHTS AND FOND MEMORIES

GENEROSITY AND LOVE
GENEROSITY
ONE LOST SHEEP
"I" STANDS ALONE
ME
HATERS
SOUTHERN HOSPITALITY
CROWN
NARD
THE ANOINTING
MARY'S GIFT
LASTING FRAGRANCE

FAITH AND HOPE
LUCK
VIRGIN
MARY'S BABY BOY
FISHING
HUNGRY FOLKS
STAIRCASE
SURPRISES
DOUBTS
MY MECHANIC
SPILL

TRUST AND FORGIVENESS
TRUST
SOMETHING GOOD
FORGIVE
DISCLAIMER
COME DOWN – MAKE HASTE
23B
BENT AND BRUISED
ZINGERS
WORDS
LET'S TALK
GRACE
GRACEFUL DEFIANCE
DESIRE
REGRETS

Water has memories
Always trying to get back
To it's beginning.

Stream, river or lake
water always finds a way
Pushing to the sea.

Structured Thoughts
And Fond Memories

Listen boys + learn
Wolves, eagles + humming birds
They have much to teach.

GENEROSITY

Where can I get some?
I see folks who have a lot
They seem so happy.

What am I missing?
Joyful giving to others.
Where does one learn that?

Values like giving
come from people we respect.
Learned by example.

Generosity!
"How can I help you today?"
"I am here for you!"

Where can I invest
to do some good for mankind?
How to use my time?

Start with prayerful thought.
Understand God's plan for you.
Generosity!

A full life well lived
will always be about love.
God is love! You too?

2 Corinthians 9:6-9

ONE LOST SHEEP

She just wandered off!
What am I going to do?
I've got a whole herd!

Maybe she'll come back.
I think she was pretty small.
No big loss – maybe?

What would Jesus do?
Oh my! Where did that come from?
We're both good shepherds.

My calling is care.
I must go now and find her.
Small does not matter!

"God, protect my flock,
as you have protected me,
that this precious one

may return to me,
held dear, as you hold your flock
lovingly in grace."

John 10:14-18

"I" STANDS ALONE

"I" stands by itself
I will always stand alone.
"We" stands together.

I - easy to spot
I want, I need, I'm so bored
Yes, it's about ME!

We - easy to spot
We plan, we work together
How to get to "we"?

Learn the basic rules!
How do couples become "we"?
Growing together!

Picking the right fight!
Never having to win fights!
Listening works best.

This poem is derived from Appendix A

ME

It's all about me!
Of course, it's all about me.
It's always been ME!

Text while I'm driving.
Speed past other cars – big deal!
Max my credit cards.

Life - like a cherry.
No responsibilities!
Pretty good deal – huh?

There's something missing.
What has possibly gone wrong?
I'm not so happy.

My friends come and go,
don't have much to talk about.
They think I'm boring.

Maybe there's reason
to think it's not about me.
Paying it forward.

Selflessness – oh my!
Give a little – get a lot!
See what comes to roost.

HATERS

When we don't agree
about important issues
it is not hateful.

Any discussion
about moral dilemmas
brings hot emotions!

Are we a nation
where the rule of law prevails,
since our nations start?

Those who disagree
call us haters to our face!
Why has hate become

the easy way out?
I'm right and you are so wrong!
What are we missing?

Evil, vile acts
are filled with hate from the start,
planned to bring response.

Hate's such a strong word.
Better - eyes and ears open,
see and hear both sides.

SOUTHERN HOSPITALITY

So nice to see y'all.
Welcome darlin', come this way.
Y'all sit right down now.

I'm Karen, your host.
Hon, coffee to get goin'?
Happy y'all are here.

I've got a surprise.
Our guests are same as family!
Enjoy each other!

We got one burner!
Two waiters didn't show up
so relax a bit.

How y'all like your grits?
Biscuits and gravy real soon,
eggs, round the corner!

"Karen, we thank you."
Darlin', you deserve the best.
Now, coffee refill?

CROWN

Whose neck can shoulder
a crown that weighs a whopping
seventy-five pounds?

I'll give you a hint
his first name begins with – d
He bore Israel!

Ha! Is that so much?
I know a very strong man
his name starts with – j

He bares all our sins.
Both are way strong, no doubting.
No need to choose lots.

God did not choose one.
Through the ages He gave both
his blessings and love.

1 Chronicles 2:1-2

NARD

Martha, get the nard,
I may want it for a guest.
Coming to dinner?

He raised a dead soul!
Our brother, once dead now lives!
Lazarus – he lives!

A true miracle.
Raised up by a Messiah.
We can anoint him.

Bring the jar of nard.
The whole flask? A year's wages!
He's the Messiah!

John 12:1-8

THE ANNOINTING

Martha greeted Him,
sister of raised Lazarus,
welcomed in to rest.

Simon the leper
offered his home to Jesus.
Bethany rest stop.

They rested and dined.
All gathered in gratitude.
Lazarus, now lives!

Mary found the oil.
Best oriental perfume,
purchased at great cost.

Alabaster jar
Fragile as rosebud petals.
Broken – anointing!

Matthew 26:6-13

MARY'S GIFT

Mary – a sinner
knelt at the feet of Jesus
grateful for His works.

Broke the fragile flask
pouring the precious nard oil
anointing His feet.

Using her long hair,
her most precious ornament,
Mary now believed.

House filled with fragrance.
A beautiful gift of love,
on His path foretold.

Mark 14:3-9

LASTING FRAGRANCE

He soon departed
Grateful home – filled with fragrance,
for Jesus as well.

To Jerusalem.
Betrayed, tried, jail and the cross,
with sweet nard fragrance.

The people he passed
on the path that was foretold
caught this fragrant scent.

Imagine standing,
seeing Christ betrayed and tried.
What would you believe?

LUCK

What's the deal with luck?
Some seem to have lots of it,
maybe the good kind

or the plague of bad.
Got two or more long-time friends?
Someone who loves you?

Lost a job or worse?
Where to turn when despair hits.
How about some prayer?

Know that God has plans
to prosper and not harm you,
a future and hope.

Call on Him and see.
Seeking Him with all your heart.
Believe that you are

held close for all time.
Just bits of luck or God's plan?
Faith holds the answer.

VIRGIN

It seems that everyone
wants three to five years
of experience.

Except God, that is
He looks for one willing
to try something new.

God waited to choose.
No experience needed.
Mary was perfect!

How does God know me?
Trembling with fear and with dread,
Mary cried out loud.

Hear the angels call.
Behold, you are in favor.
You shall bear God's son.

Luke 1:26-35

MARY'S BABY BOY

Mary did you know
your boy would walk on water?
God's great miracle.

Mary did you know
your boy would heal a blind man?
Mary did you know

that your baby boy
would become the messiah?
God's gift to mankind!

How could she have known,
God's promise to her that night?
In all creation,

Mary was chosen.
The Lord of all creation
her son forever!

This poem is derived from the song
"Mary did you know"

FISHING

All night not a fish!
Simon, I think we got skunked.
James, help me row in.

Oh, Master's coming!
Why the long faces? Bad Catch?
Not a single fish.

May I come aboard?
Let's sail out to deep water.
Master, as you wish.

Letting out the nets,
Master - no luck, Simon sighed.
Try the other side.

But Master....as the
nets were hauled, let down again.
Soon the nets were full!

Master, miracle!!
Join me on my fishing quest.
Let's go catch men's souls!

Luke 5:1-11

HUNGRY FOLKS

A big crowd had come
expecting a festival.
Hungry and restless.

No food, no wine...hmm.
Bad karma – got ideas?
Andrew spied a boy

with some bread and fish.
Enough to feed one family.
Bring them for blessing!

Pass it – they're waiting!
With thanksgiving all were fed.
Enough left over

to feed the whole crowd
again. Fed and wondering,
who is this teacher?

Let's make him our king.
We will have plenty always!
Blinded by God's gifts.

Luke 9:12-17

STAIRCASE

Between life and death
there is a sacred staircase
that spans some distance.

Though sometimes the space
between is just one small step.
A baby soon lost.

Who can predict life?
Not you, not me, only God!
His plan for us lives!

Faith, trust, hope and love.
Life well lived, small or large steps.
Rest in God's family.

Luke 20:3-4

SURPRISES

Surprises! Prepared?
Brace for life's impact! Ready?
Some are easy ones.

Winter's coming soon,
Firewood chopped, bucked and stacked?
Cold snap – no surprise!

Lamps all filled with oil,
ready to be a bright light
along a friend's path?

Some are tougher ones.
Big surprises that matter!
Life or death maybe.

In whom do you trust?
Prepared for eternity?
Eternity! What?

Faith promises help.
God always has our backside.
Surprise? Perhaps not.

Matthew 25:1-12

DOUBTS

What should I believe?
I hear many arguments.
See it – believe it!

But faith we can't "see".
Only the results of faith.
Doubt is natural.

Tests of faith bring doubts.
Strength in faith builds, one by one
bricks in life's houses.

Finish life's long race.
Fight doubt when it comes to pass.
Faith holds the answer.

John 1:2-7 / 2 Timothy 4:7-8

MY MECHANIC

My mechanic rocks!
I met him as a baby,
a close family friend.

He welcomed me in,
a part of those he helps out,
always there to help!

He had plans for me.
I hardly paid attention.
He was always there!

When I turned twelve years,
I thanked him for all his help.
He invited me,

to learn his story,
to read his old manual
so I could help too!

I use his old book
daily to learn more and more.
It's part of my life.

SPILL

One day death will tip
over your glass full of life
and it will spill out.

The earth will open
it's mouth and be satisfied
for a brief moment.

A gulp and a chomp.
One after another – gone!
What are we here for?

Do we have purpose,
or just the tipping glasses?
Gone for good – or not.

Where are we headed?
Well, that depends – maybe hell
or heaven – God knows!

Do you confess sin?
Do you accept Christ as Lord?
The body will fail

the spirit lives on!
Pick it! Death or lasting life.
Prepare – it's our choice!

2 Samuel 14:14

TRUST

I promise to trust
when I'm lonely and alone,
I want to see you.

I promise to trust
when tempted to be selfish,
I will hear you then.

I promise to trust
when I'm rushed and running fast,
You will slow me down.

When I forget you
I know you are there for me!
I promise to trust.

I am in your hands.
I am secure and safe there
trusting in my God!

Whatever my lot
You have taught me to say, it
is well with my soul.

This poem was derived from Appendix B

SOMETHING GOOD

Where am I today
on my journey to the feast?
Can I find a way,

step by step singing,
I will lift up my eyes to
the hills and see God?

We are all pilgrims,
stumbling along step by step
so sing from the heart!

Find your melody!
"Good is going to happen,"
trusting in your faith.

God meets you right there
catching us when we stumble,
grace ever-lasting!

Where does help come from?
From the Lord above, who made
heaven and earth sing!

Psalm 121

FORGIVE

How tough is that word?
Forgive! What does that word mean?
Let go! I let go.

How does that word work?
Overlook, ignore, forget?
No forgiveness there.

Shine a light and see.
Where is the wrong and the right?
Pancakes have two sides,

no matter how thin.
Time not only heals all wounds,
it gives perspective.

Fault – ammo for guilt.
Grace – merciful peace of mind.
Mercy and grace – FREE!

Let go gracefully.
The toxins of stress flow out.
A smile from the heart.

DISCLAIMER

David wrestled a
lion and a bear - and won
Don't try this at home

Similar results
are not fully guaranteed.
What is guaranteed?

God's plan for our lives.
Trust - it's well documented.
Rejoice - live your dreams.

Lions and bears come,
we can't dodge to avoid them.
We can ask for help.

Prayer is our best spear.
Ask and it shall be given.
Seek and you will find.

Seek with all your heart
God's promise is to listen
David knew the truth!

1 Samuel 17:34-37

COME DOWN – MAKE HASTE

Here He comes – can't see!
The people all hate my tax,
never let me in.

I just want a glimpse
I'm so short, I'll never see!
I'll climb this fig tree.

Ah, good spot – for now.
Tax collectors always lose
I'm wealthy but sad.

Generosity?
Not in the taxing business.
Oh, He's coming now.

Jesus saw him there.
"Zacchaeus, come down, make haste!
Your house – I will stay

tonight!! The crowd gasped!
Zacchaeus overtaken
with joy, welcomed Him.

Humble, strong for good
he promised to repay all
those he cheated and

to give to the poor.
Pure, happy and forgiven.
Another soul saved.

Luke 19:1-10

23B

Lord is my Father
in heaven who meets my needs.
Led to still places.

He restores my soul.
He guides me along the path
which is right and good.

I exalt his name.
As I walk through deep valleys,
I fear for nothing.

He protects me then,
His arms enfold, uplift me.
He prepared a plan

for my life – I know!
He blesses every day of
my life with mercy!

My cup is so full
it overflows with His love.
Surely, his goodness

mercy, will follow
me every day of my life
until the day comes

I beg for mercy
and come to be with the Lord
in heaven always!

This poem is derived from Appendix C

BENT AND BRUISED

Down at the rope's end?
Grab the bottom of His robe.
Try to hang on tight!

He will see you there
a bent and bruised blade of grass.
Ask for his healing!

He knows every blade.
We are loved beyond measure.
Looking down to see

you hanging on tight
eyes shut, weeping, but faithful
lifted in His arms.

Matthew 12:17-21

ZINGERS

I'm sick and tired
of being sick and tired.
So much pain and stress.

A zinger feels good!
How much could a harsh word hurt?
I just need a break!

Can you help me please?
Do it yourself, just this once!
A little stress gone....

but is there a cost?
Might my words come back to bite?
Zingers get zingers,

stress building more stress.
Maybe there's a better way.
What about some help?

"Lord, I can't do this
by myself, I've proven that.
Will you help me love?"

This poem is derived from Appendix D

WORDS

Cruel words get buried
in the soul and decompose
over a lifetime.

While you slowly wait
for said words to lose their shape
sadly you deal with the stench.

Kind words get your heart.
Which are remembered longer,
cruel or kind words?

Trashed by a good friend,
every cruel word recalled
at night before sleep.

Harsh and cruel words
require the count of ten
maybe overnight!

Regrets don't cut it.
Those words bite and tear at night.
Get down on your knees.

Ask for grace, mercy
and courage to make it right.
Dull the pain and hurt.

Lessons learned last long,
life changes built from mistakes.
Mad as hell? Think twice!

Psalm 64:1-4

LET'S TALK

Can't you just text me?
I'm really busy with stuff.
Talk just takes my time!

Well, I'm missing you.
I would love to meet with you.
So much to catch up.

We don't share much now.
I remember the old days,
we talked all night long!

Laughed, cried – together!
Now we just punch our feelings
into our cell phones.

I know you're still there,
your vacation blog came through.
I'm still here for you!

GRACE

I found the best class,
prof only gives out A grades!
Wow! What's this guy's name?

They just call him Grace.
What's the subject of this class?
Philosophy One.

Students and slackers
all get the same in the end?
Hardly seems right – hmm?

How about workers?
Some work hard, some not so much.
Fair to pay the same?

Depends who's paying,
their choice, paying their money!
Generous? Maybe.

I learned about grace,
the kind that only God gives.
Not earned, not graded.

God only gives A's.
His grace and mercy for all.
Forgiven – in grace!

Ephesians 4:8-9

GRACEFUL DEFIANCE

Graceful defiance!
Stop and think about that one.
A history lesson.

Making a wrong right.
Black folks at a lunch counter
waiting to be served.

Defying what's wrong,
Little by little it worked.
Graceful defiance!

Graceful change takes time.
Evolution of thinking.
Accept – day by day!

What more can we do?
One step leads to another.
Erosion of wrongs!

The title for this poem was taken from an
interview of Brunello Cucinelli

DESIRE

Want it – go get it!
Indulge yourself – enjoy life!
Chocolate – a pound!

Credit cards – max 'em.
Why hold back – I deserve it!
Pay it back later.

Self-control? Hardly.
I'm in control – by myself!
Rules? For other folks!

No end to my wants,
that's what makes me so happy.
I think I'm happy?

But my desires,
never seem to get fulfilled.
What am I missing?

Maybe self-control.
Like a life without passion.
What is this passion?

Zealous to help friends!
Living with others in mind.
That's the desire

that endures always,
the one that will satisfy.
Desires- fulfilled!

Titus 2:11-14

REGRETS

What more could I do
to prevent this tragedy?
I weep with regret.

Not a day goes by
where grief doesn't plague my soul,
that I wonder why

has this come to me?
I'm a member of the team.
Decisions gone wrong!

I have to let go,
trusting in God's forgiveness.
One day at a time.

Jeremiah 29:11-14

TWIN BROTHERS

Identical two!
Began as one, perfect split.
Grew big, side by side.

One day it all changed.
Pushing and shoving, "I'm first".
I finished second.

Wailing and crying!
I think I'll stay put for now.
More pushing - I'm gone!

Off to the nursery.
Reunion! All better now.
Inseparable!

Same likes and dislikes.
Same friends except for the girls.
They looked like our Mom.

Married our dream girls,
two kids each seemed about right.
Sales careers for us.

Get away bike trips
Holidays - great family times.
Birthdays - no problem!

One day remembered.
One day inseparable
stopped. One gone - one stayed.

The bond is still there
renewed every night with love
"Another good day".

THE BIKE

Why do I ride bikes?
Well, it started real early,
first bike – Italian!

A ten speed hot rod
with full Campy all around,
my first dream machine!

Stress just floats away.
Some miles and all is well
at least on my rides!

Eight tours of Europe.
Never thought I'd ride the Alps.
How about Ventoux!

The most famous climbs
of Tour de France – some done twice!
I know the roads, trails

of my neighborhood
well, like visiting old friends!
Hundreds of miles!

Twice each week – the bike.
Good health and time to enjoy.
Leading rides – such fun.

Lifetime sport for all.
Big climbs in the Alps or not,
the bike brings rewards!

ACROSS A CROWDED ROOM

Jim pointed her out
across a dimly lit room.
A freshman welcome.

Her? I went for it!
Far away, she was the one!
Somehow I knew her.

We met, danced and talked.
We went for a walk and talked.
Up close she was it!

The last girl dated.
We grew, loved one another
fifty plus years now.

God's plan is so good.
A lifetime of love and care.
Blessings overflow!

NANCY

I love a sweet girl.
Nancy, my wife is her name.
Oh, since I met her

I'm just not the same
'cause I love my girl Nancy.
Oh, I love that girl!

And she loves me too,
yes, I know she loves me too!
Lives joined together.

Well darlin' we love
all the time, no matter what.
The long journey won.

All my love to you.
Fifty plus years loving you,
all my love to you!

Derived from the song "Donna"

OUR ETERNITY

Who are we but we?
Knowing "we" stands together,
my wife and my friend.

I'm a lucky boy
Fifty plus years of pure joy!
How precious each day.

The touch of your hand,
your loving smile and a wink.
Your face – love to see.

My days – yours alone.
God willing, we'll see lots more.
Happy days with you!

My youth not quite spent,
still in love – oh lucky me!
Our lives grow closer.

You've fulfilled my life.
The joy of being with you,
makes my life worthwhile.

The day we married,
my new life began to sing.
Bless you for your love.

Years keep rolling by,
joys we've shared will fade away.
Love will never fade.

Knowing someone cares,
since the day you married me,
would not change a thing.

How I loved you then.
Oh, how much I love you now.
Our eternity!

FIFTY TWO

As Sinatra sang
"It's been a very good year".
Yes, indeed it has!

Fifty two great years!
A lifetime of love and care.
Everyday in love!

Learned "we" long ago.

Always standing together.
A team from the start.

So much love to share.
Our legacy for family!
Consideration.

What can I do now
to help, to give a blessing?
Kindness paid forward.

That's your daily bread.
Your love for family and friends.
And your love for me!

All my love to you!

Happy anniversary.
Many more to come.

PARENTING

Make baby – dig in!
No experience needed.
So many unknowns!

Your castle now has
a newly crowned king or queen.
Who knows – maybe both!

New parents learn fast.
Just who's in charge anyway?
Baby learns fast too,

wants to be the boss.
Whining, tantrums – what response?
Ignore or coddle?

What worked – what didn't?
Baby learns – mom and dad learn.
Experience counts!

Learning to listen
so baby learns to listen.
Growing and bonding.

Building mutual
trust and respect, so one day
"proud to say they're ours"!

FIVE DEGREES OF FREEDOM

Bye mom, gotta run.
Drive safe, streets are still quite wet.
Freedom number four!

Parents let 'em go
in small degrees of freedom
each one a life step.

Baby starts to crawl
parents so proud and loving.
Independence starts!

Practice taking steps,
soon toddler is on his own.
Walking – soon running!

Second degree done.
Then comes a bike for Christmas.
Freedom magnified.

Too soon they're driving.
More responsibility,
only one to go.

Have we taught them well?
Ready for independence.
Fifth degree is hard!

College – decisions!
Values learned by example
run deep and last long.

All five degrees done!
Proud parents rejoice – it's done.
Their world soon awaits!

PARENT – CHILD

How can I "parent"
if you won't ever "child"?
You make it so hard!

Maybe disconnect
in talking and listening
time for each other!

Take a vacation -
electronic addiction
the curse of us all!

Tweeting on twitter
Facebook - Instagram – Snapchat
Let the brain relax!

A huge world of stuff
clogging a young child's thinking.
Influence so strong!

Eye contact – try it!
Listen and hear from the heart.
Reconnect with love!

THANKS

My dad taught me this.
"Thanks" - accepted everywhere,
universally.

No price to be paid,
freely given and taken
"Thank you" means a lot

every time spoken
Perhaps it makes someone's day.
Perfectly timed help!

I'm OK – you too!
My work – appreciated.
Energy renewed.

FAMILY

Thank God for family!
Second dad's favorite words.
Love, support always!

Family? Think bigger!
Family of Man – that's a start!
That's God's whole family.

Giving – sacrifice.
Too much to ask for loved ones?
We've got a great guide.

What did Jesus do?
Nobody asks that of us!
Just what can we do?

Kindness paid forward!
What a great habit to have.
Reward? Gratitude!

BROTHERS AND SISTERS

Dad married Mom's friend,
her daughter now our sister.
Long-time friend now sis!

The tribe is growing!
We learned powerful lessons
from parent's mistakes.

Mom remarries too.
A new sister and brother,
learning give and take.

Bonding – all equal.
All loved well beyond measure.
Grown now – children too.

A close family tree.
Lots of branches – beautiful!
Each branch with new growth!

CHURCH

I grew up in church
Sunday mornings every week!
Dad, is it church day?

Shalom, shala, tov
Peace, rest and prosperity!
The end of each week!

Sunday school too.
Friday evening fellowship.
Summer camp each year.

Best friends – met at church
Future sister, met there too.
'Twas the place to be!

Values learned endure
even if one strays away.
Deep roots stand the storms.

Wayward kids – who knows?
A caring family – or not?
Church background – maybe!

Church is a habit
Passed on to our grandchildren
All involved in church!

Just like my father,
I would like the legacy,
"Christian Gentleman".

WEEPING

Weeping is letting
a flood of emotion break
through inner safeguards.

Let sorrow flow free
don't worry about the mess
The dam overflows.

Maybe for a time,
but gradually grief subsides.
Time weakens the waves.

Sorrow, grief from loss
erupt with strong emotion
weeping questions come.

"How are you doing"?
"I'm not the same without you".
"My days are like night."

Fractions of those lost
remain intact in the soul.
Treasures to hold dear!

WASTE

Just throw it away!
And just where is this "away"?
Not in my backyard!

Then in whose backyard?
That's such a waste of my time.
Time wasters – oh my!

The worst waste of all.
Now we're getting serious.
Where does that waste go?

Your backyard or mine?
What if Facebook went away.
Wasted time is found!

Possibilities!
Create the time to create,
recycled from waste!

MOUNT LASSEN

I hardly knew ya'
Mighty Lassen dumping snow,
never said how much!

Some years way too much!
Poor Chester on her backside
caught her wrath big time!

Some years – twenty feet!
Mighty Lassen giving life.
Friends – community.

Just doing our best.
Life-long friends -all still remain!
A slice of God's plan!

HUGS

I like big bear hugs.
Hugs convey some emotion.
Bear hugs – way lots more!

Lost child found – bear hugs!
Husband, father home from war?
Bear hugs – maybe more!

Lean in hugs – air kiss,
useless social ritual.
Better – just shake hands.

Hugs- returnable!
Never a restocking charge.
Give this gift and see!

WILL BOYS BE BOYS?

Cats, dogs, bucks and rams
boars, bears, lions, wolves and man,
one thing in common.

The instinct to mate
The strongest, most powerful
The big alpha male

gets the right to mate.
So what's the big difference here
with our guilty man?

It's morality!
Not taught to other mammals,
simply taught to man!

Opportunity!
Power over other folks.
What's right and what's wrong?

Curbing that instinct.
The moral compass one's learned
for monogamy!

No moral compass?
Let power over others
guide your male instincts.

Coerce and threaten
Power tools for alpha male.
Instinct or morals?

SIMPLE PLEASURES

Footprints in the sand
Warm pastries on a cold day
Waking up – no clock!

Bear hug and a kiss
Spinning windmills in Holland
Long bike rides with friends

The wind in your hair
Skinny dipping in the surf
Sunsets while at sea

Holding hands in bed
Flying competition kites
Growing tomatoes.

Family photographs
Remembering adventures
Phone calls from old friends

Walking – holding hands
An unexpected "thank you"
Making someone smile

Recounting one's years
Seeing how God's plan has worked!
Prayers of gratitude.

ADVENTURES

Plans are half the fun!
New exciting adventures
Where to next? Let's see!

Afghanistan? No!
An African Safari?
Maybe France or Spain.

Close to home or not?
What about the USA?
Remember the tune...

See the USA
In your brand new Chevrolet.
America is

asking you to call.
See the grand old USA,
greatest land of all!

Ah, another tune.
Redwoods to Gulf stream waters,
New York to L.A.

Detroit to Houston,
Texas to the shining sea.
This land – made for us!

The grand USA!
Proud to be American
See it while you can!

A SURE WAY OUT

If you're getting tired
of paying those darn taxes
there's a sure way out.

You just have to slay
the unshaven Hercules.
He's grown bold and brave.

Takers and givers.
Lots more that take than must give!
He's got us cornered!

Hmm – the Golden Goose!
Could that bird slay Hercules?
Depends where they fight.

Pick your match with care.
California – not a chance!
Maybe Idaho?

TOUCH

When oxen stumble
and eternity reaches
to caress the earth,

discipline your hand
let heaven fall where it may.
Close your eyes and see!

Where is the power?
Certainly not in our hands.
Let it go brother.

Concern for God's plan?
Want to give Him a good laugh?
Tell Him all your plans.

Relax, life rolls on.
Keep the faith and say your prayers.
God's mercy is sure!

1 Chronicles 13:3-4, 7-10, 12-14

GIFT

A gift at no cost
is different than one that costs
a pretty penny.

Which is more pleasing.
Listen to your heart, it knows.
The best gifts are free!

Your heart knows – always!
Love, kindness, a helping hand,
memories that last.

A white elephant?
You said it wasn't too much.
You're right, it wasn't!

1 Chronicles 21:23-24

UNDIGNIFIED

How would you respond
if the Lord of the cosmos
whispered – I choose you!

David stripped down and
danced like a wild animal
He knew the whole truth.

Lions, bears – bring 'em!
I've got this trusty jawbone.
Make asses of both.

Mine, that donkey's – fright!
Dance like you're wild and crazy.
Reasons to rejoice!

2 Samuel 6:16, 20-22

ANGELS

How big are angels?
I figured they were life-size.
Now I'm not so sure.

I've been told that some
have to duck under the moon
or sit on a pin.

Don't mess up with them!
Angels may save your behind.
Did you dodge failure?

"Thank God" you scream loud.
Maybe God's angels were first,
hovering above.

Never go faster
in life or in your hot rod
than angels can fly!

1 Chronicles 21:16

LEARNING THE LYRE

Who had to endure
when he was learning to play
all those awful notes?

I feel for those sheep
no hands to cover their ears.
David's favorite thought

maybe sing along.
The two harmonized a bit.
Soon David learned notes.

Baa baa sang his sheep.
Tired, sleepy he nodded.
The sheep sighed and slept.

1 Samuel 16:16

ENGLISH PUZZLE

Start with easy ones.
There's: to, too, two and tutu
do, due and dodo.

And: moo, jew, sue, you.
Oh yea: power and mower.
Sew, doe, bow and go.

A puzzle to learn
so many words spelled funny.
Sounds make a big mess.

Tot, bought, caught and yacht
No end to the head scratchers!
And: won, done, fun, one.

More? Bait, late. Beat, beet.
They never end: what, hut, putt.
Bite, white, fight and height

No wonder we have
spelling bees for every kid.
Gotta memorize!

No "bees" in Spanish.
Each vowel has it's rightful place.
Sounds the same each time!

Maybe a new law?
Our spelling revolution!!
Who won? Maybe wun!

GENTLEMAN EXTENDS HIS HAND

Cross a crowded room
Gentleman sees her and knows
Their eyes meet - "Hi there".

Girl shy and unsure
Gentleman extends his hand
May I have this dance?

Dancing and talking
Gentleman invites her out,
Opening the door.

Romance, love and care.
Gentleman extends his hand
"Will you marry me?"

Growing together
Gentleman extends his hands
holding his beloved.

Woven together
Holding each other's hands tight
Forever in love!

WHAT REALLY MATTERS?

Nature does not care
Solo sailor lost at sea
Demise unnoticed.

Scale the highest peak
Mountains don't care either
It was always there!

Disposing of us
No harm to the universe
In time, no mark left.

What really matters?
The shared brotherhood of man
Our community!

Collaboration!
Squabbles in a veil of tears,
not bricks at windows.

Together........listen!
With both your ears and your heart.
Learning to listen.

World comes to ALL STOP!
COVID – 19, BLM
We're due for a rinse.

Make your pilgrimage
a step towards understanding.
Time together heals!

The murmur of friends
Together, just sharing love
and a glass of wine!

RAIN FOREST

Quietly walking
Winding silent forest paths
Eyes and ears alert!

Giant sentinels
sporting their green fuzzy cloaks
hang their arms above.

Inspecting, groaning
"Watch yourself, we're quite fragile".
I'm just visiting.

Fresh breeze ushers me
Hushed sounds invite me – come in!
Perched crickets chirping,

Bull frog bellowing
Singing their "come here" love songs
Suddenly quiet.....

Soon back to singing
They have seen my type before
Partners on the path.

ASEA

Ah, peace and quiet
Gliding deeper and deeper,
Air strapped to my back.

Pop the ears.....relax!
One with ancient ancestors,
Not in their food chain.

Plankton to orca,
Complex eat and be eaten
destiny ordained.

Hover motionless
The food chain comes into view,
Mussel filtering

Angel fish pecking
Moray eel watching the scene
Tiger shark cruising.

We've graduated
Now ultimate predators
Polluting their home!

Can we save the sea?
Think before tossing your trash
Sea under our care!

A KING IS KNOCKING AT YOUR DOOR

Just what would you do
if a king knocked on your door?
Would you welcome him?

Would you bow and scrape?
What if the king had been there
long waiting for you?

Just waiting for you
to welcome him open armed.
There is such a king!

He will offer you
his golden crown and his robe!
Yours for nothing more

than a welcome heart.
He offers even more – life!
Eternal life – heav'n!

That king is Jesus!
His offer to believers
is first forgiveness

for a life of sin.
Redemption and love always!
Ours for the asking.

WAVES OF GRAIN

Storms a comin' soon.
Wheat fields are getttin' ready
Grains standin', waitin'.

Sailin' on the wind
Waves rollin' across the plains
Power from heaven.

Wave and swell roll by
Look all around and you'll see
The hem of God's robe!

LONELY AND ALONE

Denied fellowship
Finding some fraternity
In his meek, old dog.

Slow graying to dust
Sitting with one who suffers
His dog knew the truth.

CAN'T DO IT ALONE

Lord I'm on my knees
Whispering just help me please
Can't do it alone.

Can't do it alone.
Always faithful always true
Blessings from my God.

FUN AND DONE

Some poems are easy.
Some are a whole lot harder,
seven syllables

or maybe just five.
How about those big long words?
One syllable long!

Scratched or schlepped,
Maybe even squirreled or schmaltzed!
How to fit 'em in?

Then there's longer ones
Big, long words to fit a poem
Let's give these a try!

Transcendentalist
Interchangeability
Handicraftsmanship

Looks like we've made it!
Have some fun, compose your own.
Fun and done - The end!

I STANDS ALONE - WE STANDS TOGETHER

By
Richard A. Shultz

A process to help develop a loving, considerate and mutually supportive relationship with your partner for life. These thoughts are meant to awaken your creative energy to find the soul in yourself and in your mate that will make each day more significant than the one before, because you have the blessing of being together. In the process you may find that your soul has melded into something unexpected - your thoughts, words and actions become "we" not "I".

"I" always stands alone. I want...., I need...., I know.... Each of these phrases, whether thought or spoken, does nothing to bring a couple together in harmony. Not that each should be a clone of the other, but that each would first think of what "I" means before it becomes spoken.

It is only when "I" wishes to become "we" that the process of real growth together can begin. When a couple begins their relationship, the over generous giving of one to the other is most often a selfish motive of give and get. It comes very easily because there is no important giving and getting. When the serious stuff of relationship starts to creep into conversation, then the process of "we" either starts or it doesn't.

Each of us know couples, both new together and together for many years, that are wrapped up in "I" and rarely see the "we", because "I" is so much easier. It takes no consideration. It causes no give and take compromise. It rejoices in it's own success. We also know couples who seem to enjoy a bond of friendship and considerate give and take that astounds their friends. How do they do it? They may hear, "Can't you show my partner how to make me happy?" The answer, of course, is NO!

The process begins by gently tipping YOUR "I" on it's side. The mental gymnastics require you to begin thinking about becoming the kind of person you want in a relationship. When "I" becomes "---" you start to think in terms of what can I do to make my mates time with me today more meaningful e.g. "where are we going?". Short term, easy to do. Long term, very tough. In fact, many couples never do come to the state of "we" because they never learned the lessons of "---". First start with yourself. Who do YOU want to become in your relationship.

If two people are very lucky and the determination to learn the lessons of "---" last long enough, a miraculous process will start to occur that is beyond their knowing and beyond their doing. One "---" begins to change little by little into a "w" and the other "---" starts to curl up to look like an "e". Each is different, but together they somehow fit. Don't ever think that this process is automatic. Distractions bombard our relationships from every angle, every day. It is only the determined duo who have learned well the "---" lessons that will eventually succeed in the life long journey of "we".

Do you know couples who, soon after marriage, succumb to the "I" mentality? It's easy to let the first steps of "we" become your last. It takes daily work to remain "we". It is a growth process that is ever changing. However, the rewards for that work are the richest in all of creation.

Here's twelve words to memorize and use on a daily basis to remind yourself of the difference between "I" and "we".

GROW TOGETHER OR GROW APART

Each day, each hour in fact, when we're together or not, we're either growing in our relationship or we're growing out of our relationship. Examine your thoughts when your mate comes to mind. Do you really think in terms of   we want...., we need..., we know....   Do others get the feeling that your first consideration is always for your partner? When it's not, do you realize it?

PICK YOUR FIGHT

There will always be fundamental differences between people. It makes no difference whether that other person is a friend, a co-worker or your life partner. Cultural differences can be devastating to "we"and take an extraordinary devotion that blocks out the negative noises of friends and relatives. Other differences - child discipline, spiritual growth, use of combined resources (money), family relations, etc. etc. can cause divisions in a newly developing "we" that will threaten the whole process.

Early on in your "we" path, learn to communicate clearly those deep seated beliefs and values that you feel are not now ready for compromise.   Even if it is just a "feeling", take the time to begin building a level of understanding with your partner.   These differences never stop. In fact, new unexpected ones come into our lives as we grow and mature. It's how these differences are handled that sustains "we".

NEVER HAVE TO WIN

Can you recall a couple who began a disagreement over something quite insignificant and because of each person's "I", the disagreement escalated into an argument and then into hurting words - all for the need to win.

Never let that trap come into your life. When you're tired, worn out, stressed, you will be tested. It's very easy to let emotions of the moment get in the way of "we".   Practice giving in all things, especially winning. You will soon find that "win-win" is an expanded version of "we". Very few disagreements require immediate resolution. Bite your tongue, sleep on it. You'll probably find new value in your partner's position.

There are many fundamental practical approaches to most every difference (don't forget the "fight" stuff, that's the most important and will certainly take the most work). Here are a few suggestions.

1. Money - each person gets an allowance to spend as they wish without negative feedback from the other. All other expenditures are agreed on. This may be toughest "we" for a couple to develop. It may unknowingly be in the category of "fight". Figure that out early.

2. Spiritual Growth- Is church life important, both to the couple and to the fundamental values to be instilled in the children? Don't neglect this one as outside influence can be heavy. A church life together reinforces "we" better than any other positive influence life has to offer.

3. Free Time - Do you agree about how time together should be spent? High energy, low key? Do you agree about "get togethers" with each other's relatives?   This one will change as your life together grows. Talk about it.

These are just a few "thinking points" to get your process started. You will find many areas that do not mesh well with your life partner. Communication and consideration with a fundamental "we" behind every thought and word is often the key to success.

A last, but very important thought. If you will accept God into your life, you will have a daily partner and counselor in your daily walk to develop and sustain "we". That counselor, His son, is the Savior Jesus Christ. Through daily prayer together, whether silent or spoken, you will find that you can transfer your insurmountable, unresolvable obstacles and problems to Jesus. He will take on your burden and never let you down. He is forever faithful. He may not provide the answer you are looking for at the moment, but He will provide the answer that is best for you for your life. As the Bible says, It is important to be very still and listen for God's answer. He will always be there for you, I know!

 May God bless and sustain you on your path together.

NOTE FOR GUYS ONLY: Capitalize on a basic difference between most men and women. Women are natural nurture people, men generally are not. Therefore figure out, as best you can, what she wants (this is a rapidly changing end game, so stay alert). Do whatever it is, in advance, without being asked. Oh by the way, not that it matters, but guess what you'll get in return for doing a little advance thinking. Anything you want!! Women can't help themselves, they have to get even. The flip side of this is what women commonly mean when they say "he just doesn't get it". Gentlemen, if you do just this much, every woman I have ever discussed this with says "it's true, anything he wants".

APPENDIX B: Accompanies the poem "Trust"

PLEDGE OF TRUST

When there are times that I do not sense your presence or am not aware that you are near, I pledge to trust that:

When I'm lonely and unable to face rejection, I will trust you to be my companion.

When I'm tempted to consider my needs first, I trust you will keep me from it.

When I'm depressed and ready to quit, I trust you will lift my spirits.

When I'm overwhelmed by the demands of the day, I trust you will give me poise and sense of purpose.

When I'm rushed and running too fast, I trust you will make me still inside.

When I forget you, I trust that you will not forget me.

When I forget others, I trust that you will prompt me to think of them.

When it seems the circumstances of life threaten to engulf me, I become occupied with what I'm going through, I forget that I am in your hands. I am secure and safe even if I forget that you have a purpose for me that involves every detail of my life.

My job is to remain faithful and to irrevocably transfer my problem so my mind is at peace and to carry on.

When you take something from me, when you remove the props I lean on, when you refuse to respond to my questions and answer my too selfish prayers – I will trust you even then.

23A

The Lord is my father in heaven who fulfills all my needs.
He wants me to slow down and smell the roses.
He leads me to quiet places to restore my soul.
He guides me along the path of what is right and good to exalt His name.

Even though I walk through the deepest valleys, I have nothing to fear for he is always with me.
His arms enfold me and his hands uplift me.

He has prepared a plan for my life which cannot be denied.
He blesses every day of my life with mercy and grace.
My cup and bowl overflow with his love.

Surely his goodness and mercy will follow me each day of my life until the day I come to his house to be with my Father in heaven forever.

ZINGERS

Understanding Women

Let's set the stage with a "real life" scenario and see how different the communication process is between men and women.

You and your wife have plans for the evening that require that you leave the house by 6PM in order to be on time for the dinner party to which you have been invited. She gets home from work about 5PM and has a whole hour to get ready to leave on time. You arrive home about 5:30PM – plenty of time to get changed and out the door on time.

Your wife asks you to get all the salad ingredients out of the frig that she has staged and put them in the cooler (for later assembly at the party). No sweat! You even remember to grab a bottle of wine without having to be reminded.

You can see that she is running a bit behind schedule, but she knows when you are scheduled to depart, so being smart, you don't say anything. At about 6PM you load the salad cooler in the car with the bottle in an appropriate container. About 6:05PM she hurries out the door and off you go. About 10 seconds later she asks "did you get the croutons". "No", you say, "you didn't say anything about croutons". She hops out of the car, runs inside and after, what seems like a long time, she comes hustling back to the car. It's now 6:08PM.

You both know that the traffic signal at the main intersection is famous for not letting all the cars through before the light turns red! You're hoping to make it. Not even close – 6PM is the worst time of day for traffic at this intersection!! You are about 10 cars back from the light as you stop and she says "You're never going to make it!!!!!!!!!!!!"

The scene is now set. She is hurried, tense and ready to explode from frustration.

What do you do or say to her zinger?

Here are five "replies" that sum up your communication options.

1. Why are you always so negative?
2. Wanna bet?
3. A stoic look straight ahead – ignoring her comment.
4. Slight affirmative head nod with a raised eyebrow, meaning "who knows".

5. I know you had a lot to do to get ready. It's OK if we're a couple of minutes late.

Which one do you pick and what are the communication ramifications?
1. A guarantee to get a zinger response from her that will further distress both of you.
2. Typical male ego response, meaning "what do you know?"
3. I'm ignoring you since you're being "snippy".
4. A nonverbal appreciation of her comment as you look at her with raised eyebrow.
5. A tension reliever, she knows how much you appreciate her and all she does.

When we have plenty of time to analyze and think about these things #4 or #5 easily pop out as the preferred response choices. Of course, we rarely have the gift of time to analyze communication situations like this, so training is the key ingredient.

<u>Let's Take A Look At Her Day Versus Your Day</u>
1. She got home at 5PM and knew that the salad ingredients needed to be staged in the frig. Chop, dice, assemble.
2. She had to get dinner ready for the four and six year old boys before the baby sitter arrived.
3. She had to unravel the tantrum that the younger boy was having with his brother over sharing a toy.
4. She remembered to replace a negative with a positive and gave both of the boys a toy that they agreed to share a few minutes later.
5. She gathered up all the clean clothes that had been thrown on the couch out of the dryer and put them in the guest bedroom.
6. She had to remember if she had worn this outfit or that outfit to a function with these people in the past.
7. She took out several outfits before deciding on one that was appropriate for this party.
8. As she was finishing dressing she remembered that she had forgotten to change from her office bra to her party bra. Undress, swap, dress!
9. She had to take off her office eye shadow, mascara and lipstick and replace with party make up.
10. She worried that you would, once again, select a shirt that was not color coordinated which would require her "kind suggestion" of a change to another shirt.
11. She worried that the baby sitter would not be on time – again! - requiring a phone call and the possibility of making her late.
12. Baby sitter arrives on time! She has to inform her about the 4 year-old needing ear drops before bed and that he does not like

it, so be gentle and loving.
13. She looks at her watch and sees it is 6:05PM and that SHE is making them late!
14. She gets in the car with a big sigh and asks about the croutons.
15. She discovers, upon entering the kitchen area that the boys are down from the table canoodling on the floor instead of finishing their dinner and the baby sitter has taken out all the stuff she needs to do her nails!
16. She spends time getting the boys back at the table and gives the sitter a "wide eyed, raised eyebrow" look on her way back out the door.
17. She gets in the car, closes her eyes and waits for a comment from you.
18. Myriad thoughts, worries and concerns: office politics, her incompetent boss, the "friend" that insulted her boys at soccer practice who will be at the party, the voluptuous beauty queen that craves male attention because her husband ignores her, the youngest one's persistent ear infection, etc. etc.

Let's Take A Look At Your Day.
1. You arrive home at 5:30PM and know that you have 30 minutes until you depart for the party.
2. You check your personal email on your I Pad.
3. You change shirts to one you think she would approve – stripes not plaid!
4. You grab the bottle of wine, without having to be reminded.
5. You assemble the salad ingredients in the cooler as requested.
6. About 6PM you load the car and wait for her.

So why did she throw out the zinger when you missed the traffic signal "green".

Her Tea Kettle versus Your Tea Kettle
If you make the mistake and assume that she was aiming the zinger at you, then you may well respond with option #1. However, if you understand that her tea kettle has been on the low to medium burner since 5PM and that at precisely 6:07PM (at the traffic signal) it started boiling and she had to release some steam or it would explode! This she did. Perhaps not to your liking, but now her tea kettle is back on simmer if you selected option #4, or better yet #5 to respond. Any of the other optional responses may have actually increased her stress and caused an explosion of words that neither of you would like in hind site.

How about this option? When she got back in the car, you could not help but notice her high stress level. As you're backing out the driveway you might say, "Honey, you look fantastic. I've always loved that outfit. Thanks for getting everything done. It'll be OK if we're a few minutes late". Do you think she would have let off steam with the zinger at the signal? Of course not. You took the steam level down so far with those loving comments, that at the signal she might choose to say "nice shirt, that looks good on you".

This little exercise is meant to accomplish one goal! If we, as husbands, learn to think before we open our mouths we would be way, way ahead. Here's the take away: DON'T LET MALE EGO GET IN THE WAY OF KEEPING YOUR MOUTH SHUT.

If men would learn, by practice, to listen not only with their ears, but also with their heart, the male ego problem solves itself.

Here are a few random thoughts on the needs hierarchy of your wife.

Security: This is the first and foremost basic need of your wife. Where does she (and children if applicable) fit on your needs ladder? Does she know, beyond any doubt, that she is in first place on this ladder? That you always have her back. That she knows she can rely on you as a full partner in your marriage? Your first priority with money is family security!

Appreciation: Do you tell her how much you appreciate all she does every day for you and the kids? Do you show it by helping with stuff that can ease her burden and lower her stress level? Do you genuinely listen when she talks about her "day".

Love: Does she know how much you love her? Do you tell her and show her by your daily actions that "she is the one" you long to be with above all others by gentle, kind words and loving gestures. A loving hug with a long look into her eyes and a gentle kiss at just the right moment will bring rewards beyond your dreams!

Here is a concise needs hierarchy of husbands.
Food: Self explanatory
Sex: Self explanatory

These needs are sometimes reversed.

Made in the USA
Columbia, SC
22 November 2021